Earth Day

A Buddy Book
by
Julie Murray

VISIT US AT
www.abdopublishing.com

Published by ABDO Publishing Company, PO Box 398166, Minneapolis, Minnesota 55439.

Copyright © 2014 by Abdo Consulting Group, Inc. International copyrights reserved in all countries. No part of this book may be reproduced in any form without written permission from the publisher. Buddy Books™ is a trademark and logo of ABDO Publishing Company.

Printed in the United States of America, North Mankato, Minnesota.
092013
012014

PRINTED ON RECYCLED PAPER

Coordinating Series Editor: Rochelle Baltzer
Editor: Sarah Tieck
Contributing Editors: Megan M. Gunderson, Bridget O'Brien, Marcia Zappa
Graphic Design: Denise Esner
Cover Photograph: *iStockphoto*: ©iStockphoto.com/ranplett.
Interior Photographs/Illustrations: *AP Photo*: AP Photo (p. 11), Henry Burroughs (p. 9), CWH (p. 15), Greg Gibson (p. 13), Mark Hoffman (p. 14), North Wind Picture Archives via AP Images (p. 7); *Getty Images*: NY Daily News via Getty Images (p. 17); *iStockphoto*: ©iStockphoto.com/carebott (p. 22), ©iStockphoto.com/KimberlyDeprey (p. 11); *Shutterstock*: Igor Kovalenko (p. 19), Holly Kuchera (p. 19), Brian Lasenby (p. 19), Monkey Business Images (p. 5), spirit of america (p. 21).

Library of Congress Cataloging-in-Publication Data

Murray, Julie, 1969-
  Earth day / Julie Murray.
    pages cm -- (Holidays)
  ISBN 978-1-62403-184-7
1. Earth Day--Juvenile literature. I. Title.
  GE195.5.M87 2014
  394.262--dc23
                              2013027273

Table of Contents

What Is Earth Day?

Earth Day is held on April 22 in the United States. In other countries, it may be on another date. Earth Day honors groups working to help the environment.

Earth Day reminds people to take care of our planet. People celebrate Earth Day in schools, cities, offices, and parks.

On Earth Day, people do activities to help the environment.

Saving America's Land

Around the early 1900s, the conservation movement began in the United States. People wanted to protect the country's natural resources.

The government set aside areas for national parks. It also made laws to save animals and land.

Theodore Roosevelt was president during the early conservation movement. He helped create five national parks.

The Story of Earth Day

In the 1960s, concern about the environment grew. In 1962, *Silent Spring* by Rachel Carson was printed. This book is about the dangers of pesticides.

On December 17, 1963, President Lyndon B. Johnson signed the Clean Air Act.

People began to talk about the ideas in the book. Many started thinking differently about the effects of their actions on the earth.

Environmental Movement

By the late 1960s, many Americans wanted to protect the earth. People and animals had become sick because of poor air and water quality.

Air and water pollution harm plants and animals.

At the same time, scientists were understanding more. They were seeing how pollution harmed land and water. They shared their findings, and the environmental movement grew.

Many people worked to raise awareness. By the 1970s, countries around the world were making laws to protect land and water.

Over the years, people have celebrated Earth Day at the US Capitol.

Political Power

Gaylord Nelson was part of the environmental movement. He was a US senator. He helped pass many important laws. This included banning a pesticide called DDT.

Throughout his life, Nelson helped the environment.

Starting Out

Nelson wanted to bring people together and educate them about conservation. He asked Denis Hayes to help put together the very first Earth Day.

Hayes was a student who was interested in helping the earth.

First Earth Day

The first Earth Day took place on April 22, 1970. About 20 million people from across the United States took part. Many were students. The events on this day taught people about the importance of conservation.

In New York City, New York, part of Fifth Avenue was closed for the first Earth Day.

Cause and Effect

The first Earth Day was important to the environmental movement. Because of it, the US Congress made more laws to help the earth. One of them was the Clean Air Act of 1970.

The Endangered Species Act was passed in 1973. It protects animals that are in danger of dying out.

Laws have helped save gray wolves, bald eagles, and American alligators.

Earth Day Today

Today, Earth Day is celebrated around the world. People gather and learn about environmental problems.

Students may do activities like plant trees or pick up trash. They think about planet Earth and how to care for it in the years to come.

Environmental groups hold
Earth Day events for kids.

Being Green

Today, people continue work for the environmental movement. Some use the term "green" to refer to efforts to be earth-friendly.

You can help in simple ways. Ride your bike or walk instead of riding in a car. Plant a garden. And, try not to waste water.

You can help by recycling and reusing items.

celebrate to observe a holiday with special events.

conservation (kahn-suhr-VAY-shuhn) work done to save land, water, and other natural resources.

environment the natural world, including air, water, land, and animals.

natural resources useful and valued supplies from nature.

pesticide (PEHS-tuh-side) something used to destroy pests, especially bugs.

protect (pruh-TEHKT) to guard against harm or danger.

Web Sites

To learn more about Earth Day,

visit ABDO Publishing Company online. Web sites about Earth Day are featured on our Book Links page. These links are routinely monitored and updated to provide the most current information available.

www.abdopublishing.com

Index